Murmurations

Murmurations

Clare Dwyer

Hermitage
Press

hermitagepress.org

First published in Great Britain in 2022

1

by Hermitage Press Limited Cornwall
hermitagepress.org

Printed and bound in Britain by
TJ Books Padstow, Cornwall

A CIP catalogue record for this book is available from the British Library.

Cover design: *Murmuration III*, Janis Goodman

Paperback ISBN: 9781739856854
E-book ISBN: 9781739856861

To my Dad
for his gift of curiosity.

Contents

Foreword   vi

First Wave

Solace of a Small Bird: Wren   3
Sea Song   4
Last Letter from Mars   5
Nearly Time   6
Coreopsis   7
Photograph   8
Colander   9
Honey   11
First Light   12
Keeping Safe   13

Lull

Acorn   17
Reading Homer   18
Apple   20
Sparrows   21
Two Boldly Go   22
Star Map   23
When My Daughter Left   24
Crows   25
The Wardrobe Witch   26
Decorating   27
Birthday Post   28

Second Wave

mineself   31
Fern   32
Book-ends   33
Millfield – September   34
Intimations of Mortality   35
Sleepless   36

Hubble   37
Plasticity   38
The Wood-wide Web   39

Third Wave

A Quiet Life   43
Snipe   44
Skeins   45
Spiralised   46
Caught in Amber   48
Alex Dances A Pavane   49
The Geminids   51
Murmurations   52
One for Sorrow   53
Jewelled Golitha   54
To the Other Side of Truro   55
A Murder of Crows   56
Symbiosis   57
Shadows   58
Perhaps   59
Touch   60
Unhatched   61
A Relict   62
Winter Watch   63
Ponies on Caradon Hill   64
Starlings   65

Foreword

The poems in this collection have been written from a notebook which I kept through the duration of the coronavirus pandemic. Given that I had to shield for this time, life became rather like the shadows on the cave wall of Plato's thought experiment and so, these contemplative poems, reflect my inner life of thoughts, memories, observations of the natural world and the occasional snipe flight beyond our planet.

I don't ignore the pandemic, some poems deal with it directly, but it was such a huge event and I felt so vulnerable I found it hard to give it focus. Like many people I found solace in nature and, although my garden is small, during the spring and summer of 2020, it was a busy place with the activities of birds and growing things and that is reflected in the poetry. Like many older people, I found comfort and happiness in the interiority of exploring memories, so they are here, too.

There was an awful lot of time when I was alone (with only the dog for company) and so there is introspection here. With a significant external threat, it was a time of self-examination, an exploration of aspects of myself and my inner life which one doesn't often get the time or space to indulge. Using that inner eye was both interesting and surprising and I hope that these poems convey that journey.

It was the third lockdown which many people found most difficult and that is contained in the poems which reflect my sense of isolation and gave rise to the poems which deal directly and indirectly with the pandemic.

Snipe flights are sudden, often unexpected. My poems mimic that sudden change from my inner space to the outer realms of the cosmos. I have had a fascination for the universe which surrounds us, whether exploring it through the lens of a telescope, or the physical exploration undertaken by spacecraft such as the Voyager probes and the Rover craft currently exploring Mars. I hope that these poems convey some of that awe and fascination with a different type of flight.

Clare Dwyer

First Wave

Solace of a Small Bird: Wren

I watch your clockwork motion
as you search along the wall
collecting spiders, early morning
before the brightness turns to warmth
though too late for dawn's choristry.
Evening is different, traffic stilled
your song so big for that small throat
carrying through the leeching light.
Distinct, three parts,
I count each one and smile,
it is enough,
despite these tremors
which shake the world.

Sea Song

The sharp salt-tanged siren song
caught me before I even gave
my toes up to the bubbling froth,
before the cold sea-bite
of the wave drawing back
against my legs
and the apprehension of immersion.
Before the chill satin smooth
water slipped over my shoulders
and I became a willing prisoner
of weightless freedom.
All of it was there,
in each seaweed note.

Last Letter from Mars

Opportunity Rover 2019

Ninety sols was my
life expectancy,
ninety-two earth days.
I did so much more
for you
my distant pale blue dot,
twenty-eight miles
in fourteen years.

Doing my best
I obeyed your commands,
explored these alien landscapes,
found once plentiful oceans,
tested rocks and soil and meteorites.
Recorded the transits
of Phobos and Demios.
So much.

I am tired, my battery is low,
A storm is coming.

I shall sleep now.

Nearly Time

Picnic packed, not quite ready to leave,
it's that time of lassitude
the sun still warm
on salt-tight, sand-slipped skin.
Light dances in dimples
on the calm early evening sea.
One more sandcastle?
Another cup of tea?

Shadows grow,
a cool breeze
lifts the leaves of trees
along the path
soughing, sighing
nearly time to go,
the cattle are gathering for milking,
Mother calls as the sky deepens
our slow footsteps follow her home.

Coreopsis

Its daisy flowers
orienting to the sun
from a pot
hanging on the wall
rich summer yellow,
Coreopsis, colour popping
against lichened stone,
the only plant
my dad could name.

Photograph

Black and white, slightly creased;
two girls, heads bent
a chipped enamel colander between them.
You and me shelling peas
sitting on the back doorstep,
tongues through the skin
splitting the kernel
tasting fresh, sweet.
Mum, *Don't eat too many.*
The radio playing 'Que Sera',
how good
we didn't know
what would be,
still, it is too hard
to say your name.

Colander

I

Draining everyday life
like amniotic fluid,
rebirthing memories.
Its shape distorts
like a fairground mirror
distending the past.

II

My mother had
a cream enamelled one
its chipped rim, green.
The kitchen haunted
by cooked cabbage
and laundry
boiled in the copper.

Those smells hook me back,
her back bent,
hauling wet clothes
into the sink to rinse
and steam uncurling her hair,
strands in her eyes.
She pushes it back
with a forearm,
her hands wet.

We were too adventurous
to stay clean,
coming home filthy.
Her lips would tighten,
angry tears hanging
on her lower lids.

III
My colander hangs on a hook
its holes a mirror
of spaces, gaps, losses.

Honey

Amber glow from bees
pollen-packed thighs
light caught in a jar.
The bee-sipped nectar
notes of flower flavours,
blossom in spring,
roses of summer,
early autumn's flower
the Michelmas Daisy,
dripped from honeycomb
spun, clarified,
twelve lives
to make a teaspoon.

First Light

Morning,
not yet completely light.
The vestiges of night
still heaped in corners
where colour is not
and clouds
hold on to shadows.
A gull, wings crooked,
lazy on the wind
which plays
with the ivy
along the wall.
Beside me
the delicate nostrils
of the brown dog
twitch at scents
telling her
of the world beyond
grey walls,
grey slates,
grey skies.

Keeping Safe

If I turn the light off
to save the planet,
pick up the dog poo.
Do certain things
in a certain order
then the day will be safe.

I have to remember
the dates, not forget
the appointments,
or get the times wrong.
If I can just get it right
then the day will be safe.

I need to use the right cup,
make sure they go into
the cupboard correctly
each shape alike
each colour the same,
then the day will be safe.

I mustn't let another day
slip away from me again-
sort the disorder-
keep things clean-
stay on top-
otherwise ...

Lull

Acorn

No oak tree in sight
yet, there it was
on the ground
attached to a tiny twig,
an acorn in its cup.
In my old picture books,
red and black illustrations
on coarse post-war paper
of fairies, elves and pixies
wearing the cups as hats,
the nuts roasted,
an autumn feast.

A perfect contrast,
the glossy smoothness
of the seed, the ribbled
raised roughness of the cup.
A bird's breakfast?
Dropped in flight
a momentary loss
of concentration,
falling by my back door
to spark a chain of thought.

Reading Homer

I

Of all people you chose Paris,
handsome, self-seeking, slippery.
Inevitable he would
give you the apple
who could give him
the matchless Helen.
His vanity and yours Goddess
let loose ten years
of countless deaths
and the fall of Troy.

II

There you sit,
sulking before
your long-prowed ships,
god-like, swift-footed Achilles,
the playground quarrel,
which stole your prize,
the girl, human unmade.
How many men died
for your wounded pride,
for your vanity?
Foremost,
your beautiful lover,
sacrificed
on the altar of self.

III

Nine times
around the walls
of Troy, brave Hector,
tied by the ankles
to your chariot,
smashing his body
to appease your guilt-anger,
until you finally gave
him rest at
Priam's plea.

IV

Your death followed
not in some great fight,
but ingloriously,
an arrow from Paris
through your heel
by the Skaian gate.
Perfect warrior marred
by blood and dust,
foretold.

Apple

This apple smells
of summer's past,
sweet honey-warm days
stretching into evening
to the droning of bees,
when the colours are
fawn, mauve and gold
at the edges of fields.
Sun-coloured, sun-warmed, sun-tasting
with the crispness
of coming autumn.

Sparrows

They grew up around me
last year's chicks
now nesting in the eaves,
not taking flight
at my periodic forays
into the garden
to loosen my legs
from spending time sitting
sewing masks for family.
Twittering they forage
taking the Valerian's
setting seeds on the wall,
darting in and out of the apple tree.
These little brown birds
scarcely noticed, unremarked
with intricate, beautiful
feather patterns,
accompany my locked down life.

Two Boldly Go

for Voyagers I&II

Two small craft have passed
the point of Heliosphere
where a turbulent tug of war
causes particles to change
the momentum of their dance.
Formed by solar winds
this protective bubble
waxes, wanes, changes shape
on our elliptical, galactic voyage.
A membrane before interstellar space
which, save for those two, small craft
is uncrossed, unknown, untravelled.

Star Map

After Don Paterson

Looking down at the screen
I turn on the star map;
a vertiginous moment
when at my feet the heavens
of the Southern Hemisphere open.

I have forgotten,
as I stand on my own
tiny patch of earth,
that I am surrounded by universe
as it expands everywhere at once

and this small blue planet
caught safe within the Heliosphere
surrounding the Solar System
hurtles through at unimaginable speed.

I cannot encompass the idea
of such vastness,
it dwarfs me to a tiny collection
of insignificant atoms.

Or that this expansion
is not into some void
but is created of itself;
explanation too deep
for my small knowledge.

And how to grasp
that perhaps,
our singular, inhabited universe
could be only one of multiples.

When My Daughter Left

we said goodbye
the world dimmed
all that remained
was a hard knot of loss
behind my breastbone
where as a baby
you laid your head

Crows

They are picking
over the clumps
of moss on the roof
sending them hurtling
to the ground.
A small oil-black feather
floats whiffling down
on the air
in payment.

The Wardrobe Witch

Light from the landing
she flies to the wall
her conical hat's wide brim,
hooked nose, jutting chin.
Mother comes, flicks the switch
the room is lit from within,
−no-one to be seen.
But I know she's waiting
for the darkened room
for the half-closing of the door
climbing up again
bringing terror as before.
Years later I recall the visceral fear
made by the shadow of the cornice
the fall of light
through the angle of the door.

Decorating

The inimitable smell of freshly glossed wood,
a combination of linseed oil
and the pungency of resin
returns me to the beginning
of each new school year.
Classrooms newly painted,
all cream above the brown glazed bricks
reaching halfway up the wall.
Tall windows above
almost to the ceiling
showing only grey sky
interspersed with tree-tops
black laced fingers,
silhouetted rooks,
no views to distract
the learning child.
And the toilets outside,
bitter in winter,
salt-smelling with a urine tang.
Washing my hands in water
so cold it felt like burning.
The hours I spent dreaming
into that sky, through those trees
accompanied by the smell of new paint.

Birthday Post

Through the letterbox they come,
a rapid flutter
like a flock of sparrows
and fall to the doormat.
Each one from my children
says something about them,
a lot about me,
everything about us.
My grandchildren
all different,
Ewan's tall spikey letters
exactly like his father's.
Holly's, bold and beautiful.
Elliott's, pen pressed hard
in exactitude.
Fleur, six hearts
on her sleeve.
Jen's careful wonky letters
and baby Alice's
crayon scribble.
Each carries
their own portion of love
along with my DNA.

Second Wave

mineself

That moment, when the module
separates from the mothership,
embarks on its own journey
is akin to that moment
when a child
has self-recognition.
Though grandad's girl
Alice is just herself,
holding up a small pink
definite hand,
I do it mineself.

Aside from the me
which belongs to others
are the spaces in-between
where I keep myself.
In those scraps of time
where thought flies
unencumbered.
Not voids,
such as those
down the back of the sofa.

My favourite space
is when my mind
rolls slowly on the edge of sleep
and words burst like bubbles
in the surf
and I catch the one that fell
from an idea
which turns to air by morning.

Fern

The curl of new ferns
arch down to the furled tip
looking like a dragon's head.

Fern-filled bosky glade
Titania's bower
a place of revels,
or to sleep secreted.

Turning secluded corners
to romantic Victorian dells.

Fronded fans
to cool the living god
that was Pharaoh.

Leaf, not leaf,
spore, not seed.
Fibonacci sequence
waving in the breeze
a sea of green.
Ancient precursor
of trees, life cycle
unchanged since
the earth was young.

Book-ends

Dawn pigeons set free
explode into the sky
a chrysanthemum firework of wings
shaded white through black
in the tumbling twisting flock.

Starling murmurations
form, dissolve, shape-shift,
wings rattle, a waterfall of sound
across a sky of falling light
dropping to roost.

These avian acrobatics
bookend the day's shortening journey
as winter solstice approaches.

Millfield – September

Autumn grasses gold to purple
flowed down to the river
where insects danced in a shaft of sunlight.
Over the field from tip to tip
on swaying plumes of seed heads
silver threads of spider webs,
a weightless shimmering quilt.
Crane flies rose in their spindly ballet
to music only they could hear.
My heart took flight.

Intimations of Mortality

There are spaces in my life
where family and close friends dwelt.
Time sits close on my shoulder.
I have to think, to plan, as if
the line of my life is long.
But, Covid intrudes
and my thoughts turn inward
towards the 'what if?'

Will my young remember?
Perhaps a disembodied voice
reading or singing:
a hint of scent sparking a memory
like an old postcard,
a glimpse –
then forgotten.

Sleepless

Oh sleep catch my soul
as it dizzies past
like blown snow,
or the seed of a dandelion
caught on a fretful breeze
weightless as the wind
in awful wakefulness
as the clock slowly
bleeds the night away.

Hubble

Music from the first base notes
of Galileo's heliocentric discovery,
through time, has built
in threads of observation
up to the symphony of images
captured by Hubble.
The swelling strings
of shimmering galaxies.
Rich coloured notes
run through the Pillars of Creation,
while the Horsehead Nebular
has wind instruments in full flow,
the piccolo picking out
in a glissando of notes
a melody of new blue stars
and the tuba's deep
rendition of older red ones.
These come from far too far
for our eyes' limited vision,
this music orchestrated
from the beginning of time.

Plasticity

My generation so grateful
for plastic carrier bags.
Unreliable paper ones
disintegrated in the rain,
string handles cutting into skin.
Proliferating product
of this petrochemical age.

We wore PVC,
stepped out
Bri-nylon clad
head to toe.
Slept in it, on it,
duvet, pillows,
polyester fibre-filled.
Plastic containers
for everything,
Tupperware reigned!
Plastic in the rivers,
plastic in the sea,
plastic in a gull's egg,
plastic in me.

The Wood-wide Web

The trees whisper,
a light fluttering of leaves
across the canopy.
If you put a stethoscope
to their trunks
you can hear
their beating hearts
as water pumps upward
drawn up from where roots branch.

Across the woodland
deep underground
mycelium in intricate webs
gossip to the trees,
who is sick,
who is threatened.
The trees take care
of their vulnerable.

Symbiosis from the minuscule
to the great oak, graceful beech,
prolific sycamore.
Mycelium's gossamer filaments
attached to roots pass nutrients to the trees,
sugars from photosynthesis their reward.

We have forgotten
in the name of progress
that we too thrive
on the interconnectivity of species.

Third Wave

A Quiet Life

I've got drunk on stars
danced with the moon
played a deep note
on a tarnished bassoon.
Hid my light under a bushel
found freedom to shine,
been young, naïve—
now aged like good wine.
I've given birth
I've seen the dead,
read so many words
all crammed in my head.
I've been joyously happy
and quite the reverse,
but what defines me
is reflecting in verse.

Snipe

Reeds rattle in the sharpness of the winter wind
along the dyke banks of the marsh
the dogs ahead of me along the path.
A snipe's intricate camouflage,
barred black and gold
hides it well amongst the whispering stems,
a glimpse, more luck than anything.
When feeding, that long straight beak
stabs into the grey-green estuary mud,
precise as a scalpel.

Despite the wicked cold
the dogs hurl themselves into the water,
plunge through vegetation.
A rapid chittering, a whirring explosion from cover
into sudden unexpected flight
and the excited barking of the dogs.
The snipe drops, lost in reeds
on the far bank.
We plod home wet, but curiously satisfied.

The dogs are long gone, the snipe too.
They drained the marsh,
filled the dykes
and built houses
all the way to Southminster.

Skeins

On the beach a rolling froth-topped
wave
of sickness engulfs the land

across the sand shells mark the tide
lines
of ambulances queue

people walk, enjoying time with
families
bereft and grieving.

Inland a gull soars, its belly pristine
white
swathed inert bodies

wings angled, gliding
turning
each patient takes nine staff

swooping, seeking with its saurian
eyes
just visible above masked faces.

The calm of nature consoles
people
recovering or in body-bags.

Spiralised

Since I can remember
spiral staircases find me out,
a fault of my inner-ear mechanics
creating a visceral spinning swarm
from gut to head as the ground
falls away…

Staircase the first;
To Mrs Walding's for tea in her flat above the sweet
shop, dark-haired, plump and warm, perfect for her
calling. The stair wound up and round, halfway I was
sick, stranded unable to move.
The sweet smell of chocolate frilled with bile. Lifted
and carried by my father – mother apologising all the
way.

Staircase the second;
Four flights on a spinning well, a pouring whirlpool of
children when each bell rang bringing with them a
concoction of chalk and sweat. I clung to the
bannister drowning, fighting the sense of falling. Each
step a triumph. Eventually acclimatised, I forgot how
it had felt.

Staircase the third;
On holiday in Wales, a visit to Pembroke Castle.
Musty lime mortar, damp sea-salted wind. The steep-
stepped spiral stairs a block. Our friend takes Susie,
she's three years old. Up and away they go. What if
she falls, or he trips? Fear and sickness, sickness and
fear. Second-hand vertigo.

Staircase the fourth;
Covent Garden underground, queues for the lifts in
all directions. A nasal announcement *use the emergency
stairs, the lifts are closed* – a bomb scare! The warning
phone call unheard of now. The stairs, circling,
circling, starting to spin, people passing, trotting
upward. Air blasts from each passing train with their
subterranean rumblings bring a catch of breath.
Head down on hands and knees, a treadmill
Catherine Wheel and the violence of silent tears.

Staircase the fifth;
Inigo Jones baroque staircase, an innovation for its
time, elegantly spirals upward, portrait lined. Only as
far as the fourth step in it spins out of this world, a
merry-go-round of sickness. Pinned to the wall amid
curious glances. Rescued by an attendant and my
young son.

> I no longer fight the stairs
> it's the lift for me,
> I don't like them much either
> but I can shut my eyes,
> if I did that
> with vertigo
> I should fall.

Caught in Amber

On the wall a blackbird
stripping the Ivy berries,
–but I am caught in Amber.
Spring winkles into winter,
threats of frosts are later,
–but I am caught in Amber.
Morning slowly gets lighter
evening grows ever longer,
–but I am caught in Amber.
Leaf buds on branches fatten,
rebirth about to happen,
–but I am caught in Amber.

Alex Dances A Pavane

Through the dripping Greenwich tunnel
to visit the Queen's House
built for Anne of Denmark
beloved wife of James I.
In the great hall
paved in black and white
men and women dance
in Peacock Jacobean dress.
Sweeping across the floor
swooping and dipping
like the elegant courtship
of bright Damsel flies.
The piper trickles music
like water over stones
against the fiddle's long notes,
time kept by the drum.
We applaud its ending
of bows and curtseys.
Moving among us
they choose partners,
a lady in cloth of gold
lace fishcu at her neck
curtsies to my son
holds out her hand
and with aplomb
he takes it.
Three times they
step and count,
the musicians strike up,
the graceful dance begins.
He steps and twirls,
steps and twirls
to fiddle, pipe and drum,

bows gracefully to the lady
and me so proud
of my eight-year old son.

The Geminids

Falling out
of the unconscious of sleep,
turn off the strident alarm clock.
Slowly I leave my bed,
over pyjamas I pull
joggers, hoodie, thick socks
and plod downstairs.
The dog raises her head
questioning.
Outside the chill air
brings watering eyes
which are still
only half-focussed.
I sit, the metal of the chair
bites cold against my legs.
Looking up
I see them,
a showering of light
diamonds the sky,
my mind is woken
by awe and delight.

Murmurations

During the time of plague
these murmurs of words
drifted like dust,
settled on paper
grew shapes.

Over time they twisted,
turned
made pictures,
then settled.

Sometimes they rose
flocked,
darkened the air,
merged, melded
–changed,
became charged with meaning
then settled into verse.

One for Sorrow

Snappy black and white plumage
like a Forties Spiv
it wrecked the wreath on one
of too many new graves.

The line turned pink
and she danced.

She dreamt of a daughter
smoothed her bump
and counted magpies.

Growing up with four brothers
too many boys she thought.

Taking a cloth to her
old christening mug
making it shine.

She gave birth at sunrise,
grey clouds were tipped with gold.

She took her baby
to lay flowers
on her mother's grave.

Jewelled Golitha

At a distance the water
has the muted sheen of hematite,
move closer as it hurtles over the falls
with the transparency of peridot.
Late winter sun catches
citrine yellow droplets
returning to amethyst depths.

Water in movement calms,
quiets turbulent thought
jewels the senses,
giving emotions reign.
We are drawn in,
absorbed into its otherness
becoming ourselves elemental.

To the Other Side of Truro

The road bounded by trees
winds down to Bodmin.
Rail and river weave
and meet and leave.
A train passes
in a timpani clatter
of glinting windows.
Swinging through roundabouts
the road climbs towards Clay country,
scrubby fields, wind-whipped hedges.
The Belted Galloways graze,
memory's touchstone
of another country.
Windmills, alien sculptures
with great naked wings
scythe through the wind
studding the landscape.
A turn down a narrow lane
of stunted oak and loose grown holly.
The little girls tumble from the house
to greet us
and still,
we cannot hold each other.

A Murder of Crows

The grey granite tower
invisible in the fog.

Only the roof opposite is visible
where along the red ridge tiles

a line of twelve black crows
heads turned in secret conversation

plotting someone's downfall.
I do hope it's Boris.

Symbiosis

In the beginning
there was chalk and cheese,
North and South.
Chalk is porous,
cheese is malleable.

Time and life
have developed
in us a symbiosis,
Mum n' Dad,
Nana n' Grandad.
Infused,
each with the other.

Shadows

Inside shielding walls realities fade,
flickering pixels invade
with heartrending scenes,
shadows on the walls of Plato's cave,
of the figures, a thousand deaths a day.
Each one loved, mourned,
now reduced to a shade
glimpsed in the minds
of those left behind.

I hide away in often-read books
safe in the familiar,
Homer's poems of heroes and Troy,
tales from Scherazade.
Images bubble to the surface,
blue scrubs, breathless patients,
my prince is suspended
in his adventure.

Perhaps

Go outside on a crisp cold night,
look up!
See beyond the constellations
into the milky spiral arm of light
where there are millions of stars
with orbiting planets.

Perhaps on some there is life
different to our own
where live the evolved
descendants of dinosaurs?
Mycellium who through
intricate webs rule
green worlds in delicate balance.
Maybe there are insect worlds
of rigidly structured social societies.

But, comes the thought
that we are all there is
in the vastness of the universe.

How sad then
that we stand at the brink,
and our beautiful blue planet?
Yet another
brown lifeless world.

Touch

After Dan Gerber

Often I imagine the earth
with all the empty spaces between us
as negative electrons repel each other,
so no touch is real.
All the elements
we are conjured from
were born when the universe was young
and time had not
fixed all things
to the ticking of a clock.
Time and space
by the slip of an equation
became Spacetime,
bent gravity
and I cannot touch you,
nor you, me,
because of the space between us.

Unhatched

Curled like a bird
the fossilised embryo
millions of years
below China's surface
says that the egg came first.
What caught you
so you never hatched?
Never roamed the earth
lived out your life?

Some people are like that
who fossilise at an early age
trapped forever by circumstance
potential undeveloped.
What music could you have made?
What words might have flowed from you?
Caught by life,
Unhatched.

A Relict

In a care home,
her world diminished to one room.
Memories laid down in stratified layers;
how she danced with her sisters,
stories of her parents,
training as a nurse,
clear and bright
as a polished ammonite.

But the tales of her nephews' youthful adventures,
once well-worn grooves
are now gone.
First went the detail,
then the substance,
lost to the four winds.

Dementia leaves foundations,
the deep ploughing of the illness
destroys the surface material.
Her quick dry wit eroded
through confusion and fear.

Married for over forty years
she talks distantly of her husband,
He was a lovely chap,
she says,
But I didn't have him for long.

Winter Watch

The stark winter fingers
of trees grow fuzzy
with fattening buds—
too soon! January
is not yet over
and the month
still has teeth.

Between weeks
of murky mizzle
have been days
sharp and bright
where butterflies emerge
confused by light
and unseasonal warmth.

Even the birds
cannot grasp this winter,
already flitting, fighting
after a mate
through garden shrubs.

One stalwart plant
is still pushing out
thin stems of
pure white flowers.

Where are the ice-patterns
on the windowpanes?
Snow deep enough
to bring out sleds?

Things of hearsay
consigned to memory.

Ponies on Caradon Hill

It is hat weather,
eye-tearing wind
lifts the long guard hairs
on the ponies' winter coats
as they blow soft clouds
of steam, dewing their muzzles.
They shelter under wind-shaped thorn trees
a black tangled lace of branches
against winter clouds.
A motley herd, all colours,
they are uncurious
as we walk by.
Three face outward,
sentinels for the grazing others,
some with leggy foals
from last spring's birthing.
Soft-eyed with long lashes
for protection against the moorland rain,
though un-needed today
as the sun sends shafts of light
across distant fields and trees
backlit by pale gold.
The odd bloom of gorse
sparks against the dark hill
tinges the musty scent of horse.
We pass – and let free the dog again.

Starlings

Memories flocking, weaving,
they merge and meld,
fluttering down
in a steady pouring from the past
loosed by a fragment of fabric.

When young
she looked like Ingrid Bergman
in a coat which fell in soft folds
the colour of old brick.
Her grey tailored suit
with a white pin tucked blouse
delicately embroidered
and smart court shoes.

This fabric shimmers,
movement
green to gold,
midnight dark.
The frock
hugged her figure
a huge fanned bow
at the back
just on the waist.
It could have
been made by Dior
instead of by her.
Her starling dress
we called it
though she didn't
like starlings.

Acknowledgements

Whilst writing is a singularly solitary job, I have not been without a great deal of help and support and these acknowledgements are my thanks to those, without whom, this collection of poems would never have broken cover.

So, thank you to ...

My parents, who carefully left books around for me and my siblings to discover, who never treated poetry as if it was something rarefied but was part of the everyday. They would have been really proud of this book and it is the only sad note that they are no longer here to read and enjoy it.

To each of the Liskeard Poets, past and present, who have been an inspiration and an incredibly valuable sounding board each month for the last ten years. Each of you has bought a different perspective and have always been so positive and supportive.

To my 'poetry buddy' Anna Chorlton, for sharing her poetry books and whose unfailing support has been greatly appreciated.

Jackie Harding and Hillary Puttock for those wonderful two years at Truro leaning about form, structure and how poetry worked (amongst many other valuable things). I can never thank you enough.

Dr. Miriam Darlington, whose supervisory sessions during my M.A. were stretching, thought provoking and an absolute joy, and for her continuing support and friendship.

Dr. Min Wild for letting me sit in on her Poetry and Philosophy, module which was inspiring and an education.

Drs Ben Smith and Mark Leahy for their unfailing patience with my snipe flights and their enriching teaching.

My family, for their love and support, especially my husband Mike who coped with my meltdowns with unfailing good humour and care.

Dr. Catriona Thorton without whose care I would not have made it this far.

Anyone I may have inadvertently missed, I apologise, but you have my heartfelt thanks.

Finally, to my publisher and the team at Hermitage Press, for liking these poems enough to turn them into book form.